MW01228382

A BREATH OF AFRICA

To Jo
An artist in so many ways
with gratitude
Lysa

A BREATH OF AFRICA
HAIKU

by
Lysa Collins

GRANVILLE ISLAND
PUBLISHING

Publisher's Cataloging-in-Publication Data

Collins, Lysa, author.
A Breath of Africa : haiku / by Lysa Collins.
Vancouver, BC: Granville Island Publishing, 2020.
ISBN 978-1-989467-16-9 (Hardcover) | 978-1-989467-13-8 (pbk.)
LCSH Africa—Poetry | Africa—Description and travel—Poetry. |
Canadian poetry—Women authors. | Canadian poetry—20th century. |
Bisac Poetry / Subjects & Themes / Places
LCC PR9199.3.C631 B74 2020 | DDC 811.6—dc23

Front cover image by Paul Hampton
Back cover image by Martin Pateman-Lewis

Book designer: Omar Gallegos

Granville Island Publishing Ltd.
212 – 1656 Duranleau St. Granville Island
Vancouver, BC, Canada V6H 3S4

604-688-0320 / 1-877-688-0320
info@granvilleislandpublishing.com
www.granvilleislandpublishing.com

Printed in Canada on recycled paper

for you, with love . . .

Foreword

a lion's roar
wraps the veldt
in stillness

Lysa Collins

For many readers of haiku poetry, Africa is an exotic and distant place. I had the privilege of living in Ghana when I was a child, and of visiting nearby countries, but my memories are from long ago. So, for me, Africa still seems exotic and distant, even if I can still picture a huge centipede in our driveway in Kumasi, or recall a sub-Saharan native running his fingers over my head because he had never seen straight hair. I'd love to go back.

But of course, there are many Africas. Those of us in the Americas, Europe, and elsewhere, too easily lump the entire continent into one diminishing label, like thinking it's enough to call Albert Einstein and Nelson Mandela 'people'. Using the term 'Africa' too easily sweeps away the varied culture and geography and the many languages and dialects into one dismissive lump. You can converse in more than 1,500 languages — the highest linguistic diversity on the planet. As with its diversity of animal species, the continent's variety of languages serves as a metaphor for every other kind of diversity possible throughout these extraordinary lands. We all know about giraffes and gorillas, but did you know you can go downhill skiing in Morocco, Algeria, Lesotho, or South Africa? We can also explore parched and colorful deserts in the vast Sahara or Kalahari, investigate jungles and glaciers (both are shrinking), coasts and mountains, savannas and rivers, pyramids and penguins, shopping malls and shanties and feel safe in some cities, unsafe in others.

The stamp of colonialism runs deep, but the roots of native culture run far deeper. Europeans in the past called Africa the 'dark continent', which meant, some said, that it was unknown. In many ways the continent is still dark to Westerners, and we do not help to penetrate or appreciate its mysteries by referring to the entire continent all at once. We don't need to know "Africa". We need to know the many places and faces of Namibia, Sierra Leone and Madagascar — and focus more closely on the rich details awaiting our discovery. What we can get out of Africa is subtlety, variety, and diversity of every aspect of its cultures, languages, botany, and wildlife.

And yet, where do we start? How do we apprehend the mystery of Africa's individual countries and their many subcultures, let alone the entire continent? The answer begins with understanding small parts. And that, I think, is what this book offers. It's a visitor's view, and every vacationer or sightseer has valid experiences — they are a door to deeper understanding. What follows here are poems Lysa Collins has written about her visits to South Africa, Botswana, Zimbabwe, Zambia, Tanzania, and Kenya and they give you a taste, not of the entire continent, but of small parts of it —

the flora and fauna of personal experiences that can enrich readers by their otherness — and also by their sameness.

After the author takes a prop plane to begin her adventure, this book unfolds with focuses on specific locations. These locales provide structure for sequences of poems on the Kalahari Desert, the Serengeti Savanna, the Ngorogoro Scrubland, the Great Rift Jungle, the Rivers of the Okavango Delta, and villages in and around Kigoma.

In *Out of Africa*, the memoir by Karen Blixen, also known as Isak Dinesen, the renowned Danish author says, "You know you are truly alive when you're living among lions." These poems by Lysa Collins show her aliveness as she visits, and seeks to understand, particular parts of Africa.

— Michael Dylan Welch
Former Vice-President
The Haiku Society of America

Contents

Zinkwazi Wind

take off
from a stretch of sand —
the pilot wets a finger

a shift of color
where the reef drops off
without me

elephant
on the airstrip —
we circle back in time

rail line to Mombasa
streaked with sand
and swallows

doum palms
and a clutter of huts —
faint thunder

bush tea —
a monitor lizard
tastes the breeze

outside my tent
the crack of branches
stills

night shadows
flit across the wall
… I should have known

Kalahari

sweep of sand
where no one goes
a small thrush, trilling

dry stream bed —
a mottled rock
takes flight

buttonquail
and a shake of seed
left behind

desert calm
the small mouse
… shivers

clothes hang abandoned
winds through the wall
blow skeleton seeds

desert night —
crosswind
and a creaking in the dunes

sheets of sand
slide down steep slopes
night holds back the stars

Serengeti

first light
edging through dry brush
into the leopard's stealth

almost heard
from a castle mound —
termites spitting mud

ancestral trail —
wisps of tamarind
reach…

salt laced clay —
the delicacy
of an eland's hoof

balmy afternoon
across the buffelgrass
a drift of quail

whiff of rain —
a wildebeest calls
and the grasslands thrum

dipping sun —
the weaver bird
sings quiet songs

moonlight
and warm winds
gather in wild gardenias

Southern Cross —
giraffes regroup
to creche their young

a lion's roar
wraps the veldt
in stillness

Ngorogoro

morning
in the water berry tree
bats hung out to dry

barefoot boys
trek to school —
        a cappella

Olduvai —
echoes in the boulders
from before there was song

peat bog —
a mudfish digs
into the past

sharp snarl
and the cackle of hyenas
drains down the gorge

scrubland —
a startle of quail
reshapes the sky

in tufted bristle grass
a cheetah cub
purrs out the afternoon

sunbeam
on a peacock pluming —
the feel of iridescence

sun setting
on the ridgeline
a walk of elephants glides in

moonrise on Lake Nakuru
a thousand flamingoes
pay no attention

night wind —
the angel's trumpet
spills a warning

Great Rift

morning sun —
a baby elephant
nudges the old marula tree

young leopard
on a low-slung branch
shifts his weight

in the twitch
of a cheetah's whisker
elegance

gorilla
in the undergrowth
… breathes for the two of us

mangrove swamp —
a machete
slits the silence

glare of sun —
on the track
an obstinacy of buffalo

fig tree
with no figs at all —
monkeys

under the mopane tree
chimpanzees and me
othering

mountain ledge —
I share celery
with a silverback

clouds brush the high veldt —
the wind shifts
to a minor key

mountain
by mountain
colobus disappear

long leaps
of the howler monkey
carry the last light home

chill wind —
the weaver bird nest
swings empty

beyond the bonfire
voices flicker
in the night

sultry dark —
a lion's chuff
thins the canvas

moonless sky —
the long talks
of old lions

Okavango Delta

Okavango Delta —
dawn climbs slowly
from rhino to rhino

with a snort
one hippo
lifts the lotus pond

heat shimmer —
among green reeds
a dugout, ghosting

egret landing on his back
the old rhinoceros
sighs

oozy mud —
black buffalo grunt
at the shutter clicks

a snapping
of enormous teeth —
the riverbank vacates

clump of hippos
napping in the shallows —
imprudently we yawn

slow stream —
hooded eyes
follow the papyrus raft

sand bar —
incoming fog
streaks with marabou screech

blood moon —
young lions roar
just for practice

Kigoma

I didn't know
how loud the lake —
dawn

sun drenched village —
grass full of sausage fruit
and one staggering elephant

broken pot
by the well
a scold of shrikes

mid afternoon
beneath the baobab
the wind and I, resting

monkeys
in the almond tree —
I put out the chair with arms

small hedgehogs huff
and tuck themselves
in separate silences

a decade on
the old blind rhino
still nuzzles at my hand

clear cut acacia —
I teeter
on the fallen years

warm wash of dusk —
among the citrus trees
a linger of nightingales

a cool breeze
coasts the tassel grass —
some things you never say

sunsets
and zebras
etch my life with leaving

Notes

Zinkwazi

i   'Zinkwazi' — refers to a beach and small town with an airfield, on the tip of Africa, where people enjoy windsurfing, kiting, etc.

ii 'doum' — a type of palm with edible fruit

Serengeti

i   'tamarind' — a tree from which the fruit pulp is used in cuisine and medicines

ii   'buffelgrass' — a long leaved native grass

iii 'Southern Cross' — a constellation prominent in the Southern Hemisphere

iv   'veldt' — African grassland dotted with some trees and shrubs

Ngorogoro

i 'water berry' — a tree with uses for every part of it, including edible berries fermented for alcoholic beverages and bark used to remedy stomach problems and diarrhea

ii 'Olduvai' — the paleoanthropological site called the 'cradle of mankind' where Mary and Louis Leakey made their famous excavations

iii 'Lake Nakuru' — a soda lake noted for its multitude of flamingoes

iv 'angel's trumpet' — another name for the hallucinogenic 'datura'

Great Rift

i 'marula' — a common tree with edible fruit

ii 'mopane' — a tree with large butterfly shaped leaves

iii 'colobus' — endangered species of mountain primates

iv 'lion's chuff' — lions can make a noise like a big sniff — not welcome near a tent

Okavango Delta

i   'hippos' — don't like to be disturbed and may easily attack

ii 'marabou' — these storks have a peculiarly loud, strident call

Kigoma

i   'lake' — Tanganyika, a large body of water nearby

ii   'sausage fruit' — when fermented, can be quite intoxicating, even to elephants

iii 'baobab' — a tree seeming to grow upside down

iv   'acacia' — native African tree, a landmark on the veldt

My sincere appreciation to all those wonderful people, close at hand and far away, who have given so generously of their time, energy, encouragement, and expertise, to assist me on my way to the publication of this book.

Acknowledgements

Acorn
Akitsu Quarterly
Asahi Haikuist Network
at the water's edge (Haiku Canada Members' Anthology 2019)
Autumn Moon Journal
The Bamboo Hut journal of English language tanshi
bottle rockets
cattails United Tanka and Haiku Society
Chrysanthemum
ephemerae
a far galaxy (Haiku Canada Members' Anthology 2018)
Four Hundred and Two Snails (Haiku Society of America Members' Anthology)
Frogpond

haiku xpressions (FreeXpresSions)
Hedgerow: a journal of small poems
The Heron's Nest
a hole in the light (Red Moon Anthology of English-
    Language Haiku 2018)
Hummingbird: Magazine of the Short Poem
International Haiku Magazine ginyu
The Mamba
Mayfly
Modern Haiku
Paper Wasp
Presence
Under the Basho
Wales Haiku Journal
Wild Plum

Thank you to all the editors and publishers of these fine publications in which my work has previously appeared.

Photo at Wild Horizons Elephant Sanctuary,
Rescue Rehabilitation and Release Centre

Lysa Collins is an environmentalist, world traveler, poet, and supporter of the Jane Goodall Institute and the African Wildlife Foundation.

She currently lives in British Columbia on the west coast of Canada, overlooking the longshore drift. She writes haiku and other short forms of poetry, which appear both in English and in translation, locally, nationally, and internationally, in a variety of print and online publications.